# Once Upon A Dream

## Dancing Shadows

Edited By Lynsey Evans

First published in Great Britain in 2024 by:

Young Writers
Remus House
Coltsfoot Drive
Peterborough
PE2 9BF
Telephone: 01733 890066
Website: www.youngwriters.co.uk

All Rights Reserved
Book Design by Ashley Janson
© Copyright Contributors 2024
Softback ISBN 978-1-83565-394-4

Printed and bound in the UK by BookPrintingUK
Website: www.bookprintinguk.com
YB0588P

# FOREWORD

Welcome Reader, to a world of dreams.

For Young Writers' latest competition, we asked our writers to dig deep into their imagination and create a poem that paints a picture of what they dream of, whether it's a make-believe world full of wonder or their aspirations for the future.

The result is this collection of fantastic poetic verse that covers a whole host of different topics. Let your mind fly away with the fairies to explore the sweet joy of candy lands, join in with a game of fantasy football, or you may even catch a glimpse of a unicorn or another mythical creature. Beware though, because even dreamland has dark corners, so you may turn a page and walk into a nightmare!

Whereas the majority of our writers chose to stick to a free verse style, others gave themselves the challenge of other techniques such as acrostics and rhyming couplets.

Each piece in this collection shows the writers' dedication and imagination – we truly believe that seeing their work in print gives them a well-deserved boost of pride, and inspires them to keep writing, so we hope to see more of their work in the future!

# CONTENTS

## Alec Reed Academy, Northolt

| | |
|---|---|
| Lariya Jeffrey-Sutherland (10) | 1 |
| Nikola Kunik (9) | 2 |
| Hayat Ahmed (10) | 3 |
| Zoe Biriya (9) | 4 |
| Khaya-Marie Corbin-Johnson (10) | 5 |
| Lilly-Mae Burton (10) | 6 |
| Jayda Blu O'Sullivan (10) | 7 |
| Kirushika Raveendran (10) | 8 |

## Antonine Primary School, Bonnybridge

| | |
|---|---|
| Aydan Tait-Crossan (9) | 9 |
| Lhouis John Flores (10) | 10 |
| Amy Love (9) | 11 |
| Aimee Burns (9) | 12 |
| Iona Sutherland (9) | 13 |
| Jessica Bell (9) | 14 |
| Lucy Noble (9) | 15 |
| Xander Cameron (8) | 16 |
| Cameron Gibson (9) | 17 |
| Hamza Riaz (9) | 18 |
| Sienna Kay (9) | 19 |
| Aaron Pittendreigh (9) | 20 |
| Kai Blain (9) | 21 |
| Kian Stevenson (9) | 22 |
| Madison Corrigan (9) | 23 |
| Kenzie Piper Wright (9) | 24 |
| Amy Callaghan (9) | 25 |
| Halle Cunningham (9) | 26 |
| Callan Logan (9) | 27 |
| Noah Charleston (9) | 28 |
| Lucy Byars (9) | 29 |
| Skye-Leigh Price (9) | 30 |

## Armoy Primary School, Ballymoney

| | |
|---|---|
| Brandon Kennedy (10) | 31 |
| Charlotte Rainey (11) | 32 |
| Sorana McCook (10) | 34 |
| Jamie Simpson (10) | 35 |
| Gracie Adams (10) | 36 |
| Sara Cushnahan (11) | 37 |
| Josh McCurdy (10) | 38 |
| Emily Knox (10) | 39 |
| Tyler Lyons (11) | 40 |
| Katie Boyle | 42 |
| Callie McCooke (9) | 43 |
| Archie McNeill (10) | 44 |
| Riley Linton (11) | 45 |
| Noah Christie (10) | 46 |
| Grace Dobbin (10) | 47 |
| Amelia Moore (9) | 48 |
| Owen Boyle (11) | 49 |
| Jessica Leeming (10) | 50 |
| Oliver McCook (11) | 51 |
| Molly Moore | 52 |
| Mason Kane (9) | 53 |
| Danny Mooney (11) | 54 |
| Carson Irvine (10) | 55 |
| Noah Johnston (10) | 56 |
| Lexi O'Lone (9) | 57 |
| William Hanna (10) | 58 |
| Macy Elder (10) | 59 |

## Braidside Integrated Primary And Nursery School, Ballymena

| | |
|---|---|
| Evie Truesdale (8) | 60 |
| Lila Dunceith (8) | 62 |
| Emilie Barr (9) | 64 |
| Shannon Payne (9) | 66 |
| Tommy Swann (9) | 67 |
| Emilie Thompson (9) | 68 |
| Liberty Stewart (9) | 69 |
| Preston Balmer (9) | 70 |
| Hallie-Mae Quigley (8) | 71 |
| Annie Corry (8) | 72 |
| Darcie Williamsam (8) | 73 |
| Erin Nelson (9) | 74 |
| Reuben Dinsmore (9) | 75 |
| Sophia Elliott (9) | 76 |
| Erin Rose (8) | 77 |
| Sophia McNeill (9) | 78 |

## Charlton House School, Bitterne Park

| | |
|---|---|
| Ella Prouton (9) | 79 |
| Keyara Minors (10) | 80 |
| Ayesha Iqbal (10) | 82 |
| Oliver Noble (10) | 83 |

## Gesher School, Pinner

| | |
|---|---|
| Ari Feldmann (9) | 84 |
| Leon Krett (9) | 85 |
| Advait Raipara (9) | 86 |
| Poppy Hass (8) | 87 |

## Glyncorrwg Primary School, Glyncorrwg

| | |
|---|---|
| Connie Lee (10) | 88 |
| Gracie Quinn (9) | 89 |
| Zak Williams (10) | 90 |
| Lucy Protheroe (10) | 91 |
| Isabel Lloyd (8) | 92 |
| Marnie Dennedy-Doyle (9) | 93 |
| Albie Williams (8) | 94 |

| | |
|---|---|
| Ollie Bufton (10) | 95 |
| Olivia Enoch (10) | 96 |
| Tabitha Meredith (9) | 97 |
| Lily White (11) | 98 |
| Kayden Walters (10) | 99 |
| Autumn-Fayy Jones (9) | 100 |
| Jackson Warlow (11) | 101 |
| Levi Woodbridge (10) | 102 |
| Sonny-Rayy Jones (10) | 103 |
| Maigan Fields (10) | 104 |
| Roshi Garrity (9) | 105 |
| Seren McCabe (9) | 106 |
| Lucy Bath (9) | 107 |
| Craig Fullerton (9) | 108 |

## Holy Cross Preparatory School, Kingston Upon Thames

| | |
|---|---|
| Luciana Diaz-Jimenez (9) | 109 |
| Alice Le Broussois (10) | 110 |
| Olanna Nwafor (10) | 111 |
| Vasundhara Bahree (9) | 112 |
| Jasmin Patel (9) | 113 |
| Raya Al-Derzi (9) | 114 |
| Amalia Vilaseco (9) | 115 |
| Lara Chakravarty (9) | 116 |
| Sophia Kim (10) | 117 |

## Northlew And Ashbury Primary Parochial CE School, Okehampton

| | |
|---|---|
| Izabella Faith-Brown (10) | 118 |
| Darcie Canham (10) | 119 |
| Arabella Porteous (10) | 120 |
| Thea Page (10) | 121 |
| Laila Chastey (9) | 122 |
| Dylan Vallance (7) | 123 |
| Casper Page (10) | 124 |
| Zac Dryden (8) | 125 |
| Oliver Cork (9) | 126 |
| Laila Dryden-Chastey (9) | 127 |

## South Moreton School, Didcot

| | |
|---|---|
| Sophie B (11) | 128 |
| Alex Ackers (10) | 130 |
| Sasha K (10) | 132 |
| Cecily Hillegonds (11) | 134 |
| James Aston (10) | 136 |
| Enid Bonsu-Dartnall (11) | 138 |
| Sonny Webster (11) | 139 |
| Jessica C (10) | 140 |
| Cameron Rayner (10) | 141 |
| Evie Bowler (10) | 142 |

## St John The Divine CE Primary School, Camberwell

| | |
|---|---|
| Kaley Joseph (6) | 144 |

## St Joseph's Primary School, Gabalfa

| | |
|---|---|
| Milena Katherine Lawrence (11) | 145 |
| Millie O'Brien (10) | 146 |
| Joanne Ifada (10) | 147 |
| Drishya Babu (10) | 148 |
| Maurycy Hebel (10) | 149 |
| Pranav Shake (10) | 150 |
| Ruby-Rose Stacey (10) | 151 |
| Alysia Jones Pleace (10) | 152 |
| Gracie Toppar (11) | 153 |

## St Mary's Catholic Primary School, Newcastle-Under-Lyme

| | |
|---|---|
| Olivia Timms (11) | 154 |
| Pita Joseph Rhys Ezekiel Daniel Smith-Tavakece (10) | 156 |
| Connor Jordan (10) | 157 |

## St Mungo's RC Primary School, Alloa

| | |
|---|---|
| Vygha Jismon (10) | 158 |
| Connor Clark (10) | 159 |
| Stephen Moore (10) | 160 |

| | |
|---|---|
| Khloe Holdsworth (10) | 161 |
| Gabriella Annabell Czarnik (10) | 162 |
| Aron Beely (10) | 163 |
| Grace Gallagher (10) | 164 |
| Olivia Hall (9) | 165 |
| Jacob Lovell (10) | 166 |
| Emmie Douglas (9) | 167 |
| Jensen McAdam (10) | 168 |
| Harry Douglas (10) | 169 |
| Nadia Ludwiczak (10) | 170 |
| Max Cassidy (10) | 171 |
| Alix Lawrie (10) | 172 |
| Lilly Kane (10) | 173 |
| Perri Starkey (10) | 174 |
| Alba Williamson (10) | 175 |
| Logan Cameron (9) | 176 |
| Kai McMorrow (10) | 177 |

## Sundon Lower School, Upper Sundon

| | |
|---|---|
| Viraaj Singh Kalsi (8) | 178 |
| Davina Dencil (7) | 179 |
| Jeevan Bhaker (8) | 180 |
| Nico Charles (9) | 181 |
| Jason Roe (8) | 182 |
| Roxanne Janas (7) | 183 |
| Saffiya Charles (9) | 184 |
| Haajer Sadiq (8) | 185 |
| Stefan Gagic (8) | 186 |
| Felix Orme (8) | 187 |
| Riya Sharma (8) | 188 |
| Mia-Rose Garland (7) | 189 |
| Harrison Martin (9) | 190 |
| James Price (7) | 191 |
| Ah'Shay Duncan (8) | 192 |

# THE POEMS

# Heartless Love

Sometimes love is like when someone's heart opens up inside,
But sometimes it can show people's true colours.
Giving second chances doesn't change anyone,
Like reading a book twice doesn't change the ending,
Or daydreaming over and over again
Doesn't change what you're thinking.
So look into my eyes
Because getting heartbroken fifteen times is no surprise,
But never change who you are,
Because everyone is different
Just like a bright shining star.
Change, whether that's good or bad,
Don't waste your breath on me,
Because there are other fish in the sea.

**Lariya Jeffrey-Sutherland (10)**
Alec Reed Academy, Northolt

# Goodnight

**G** oing to sleep is harder than I thought, since I don't dream a lot.
**O** nce I lie still in my bed, I think, goodnight, goodnight, though it does nothing.
**O** nce I close my eyes, I open them back, thinking about my future.
**D** o you know what I can do?
**N** ow I think back to myself again, goodnight, goodnight.
**I** lie still for a lot of minutes and try to sleep, but I'm still wide awake.
**G** oing to sleep for me always takes a long time.
**H** ow could you help me sleep?
**T** hen after a long time trying to sleep, I close my eyes and suddenly fall asleep.

**Nikola Kunik (9)**
Alec Reed Academy, Northolt

# Bullying

If you think bullying is cool,
Then you must be cruel.

The girl who is bald,
The lady who is old,
They both show fear,
Because you've made them burst into tears.

The boy you just tripped,
He has already been in enough conflict,
The man with the ugly scars,
He fought for his country and is one of the world games stars.

Change your ways,
Change your heart,
Because on the inside
You're a superstar!

**Hayat Ahmed (10)**
Alec Reed Academy, Northolt

# I Wish I Could Fly

I wish I could fly like a bird.
Everyone says I can't, so I'm like, I've heard that before.
I know I can skydive, but it is not the same thing.
Sometimes I wish there was no gravity so I could fly like a plane.
If I can't fly, then I will learn to fly a plane.
I know I can have other wishes, but I only want to fly.
Many people would wish this, but they would change their minds, but that's not me.

**Zoe Biriya (9)**
Alec Reed Academy, Northolt

# Midnight

Under the midnight, stars gleam so bright,
Twinkling dance fills my heart with pure delight,
In their cosmic embrace, happiness takes flight.
Midnight magic, a symphony of sheer delight.

As the clock strikes twelve, the world falls asleep,
But the stars above, their secrets keep.
They twinkle and shimmer a celestial show,
Filling my heart with happiness aglow
That grows inside my heart.

**Khaya-Marie Corbin-Johnson (10)**
Alec Reed Academy, Northolt

# I'm Not Unlucky!

Jump up and run
Let's have some fun!
I'm just a black cat
I love to sleep on mats
Some things I dislike are...

People calling me bad luck
All those people suck!
People spreading lies
That makes me sigh!

Anyway, things that I like are
Cat food of course!
Sleeping makes me happy
Playing makes me crabby at times!

Well bye-bye
Meow, meow.

**Lilly-Mae Burton (10)**
Alec Reed Academy, Northolt

# The Blossom Trees And You And Me

I can feel the breeze of the blossom trees
It's just you and me
I can feel a new future rise
That's what I can see through the door
I can see the blossom leaves
Fly down to the floor
It's the best thing I ever saw
Painting pictures of what you draw
Your eyes are blue like the seashore.

**Jayda Blu O'Sullivan (10)**
Alec Reed Academy, Northolt

# Roses

Roses are beautiful, blooming, delicate and pretty
The redness of roses calls to mind the romantic associations of the colour
Roses are red
Violets are blue
Poems express my love, you do too
When I'm with my cousin my heart feels brand new.

**Kirushika Raveendran (10)**
Alec Reed Academy, Northolt

# Winter's Home

**W** inter's home is always bright
**I** gloos so cold but not too cold for a nice warm home
**N** ature time with fun, joy and laughter
**T** rees like blossoms, fresh green grass
**E** ven though it's snowing, people like to play on Christmas Day
**R** eady for presents and movies all night for Santa in our sight.

**Aydan Tait-Crossan (9)**
Antonine Primary School, Bonnybridge

# Winter Acrostic

**W** inter day is very slippery outside
**I** n the road it's really icy and cold
**N** iamh and Steve are playing with snowballs and it's cold
**T** oday everybody knows it's cold and they're freezing
**E** very morning it's cold and freezing
**R** ight now snowy and frosty.

**Lhouis John Flores (10)**
Antonine Primary School, Bonnybridge

# Winter

**W** arm and cosy hot chocolate
**I** ce is so cold
**N** ice and comfy jammies
**T** he snowman is glistening
**E** xcited for freezing snow
**R** eady for a warm bath.

*A haiku*
Birds screaming all day
The sun is too hot for ice
Smell hot chocolate.

**Amy Love (9)**
Antonine Primary School, Bonnybridge

# Winter

**W** ake up on my cosy bed then get yummy breakfast
**I** cy ice on the roads
**N** ever wake up too early though
**T** easing people with presents is nasty though
**E** very winter breakfast is tasty
**R** eady to get my presents opened.

**Aimee Burns (9)**
Antonine Primary School, Bonnybridge

# Winter

**W** arm inside, freezing cold outside
**I** cicles starting to evolve
**N** athan and Johnathan playing in the snow
**T** emperature dropping lower than zero
**E** veryone is freezing cold
**R** ight before bed it snowed even more.

**Iona Sutherland (9)**
Antonine Primary School, Bonnybridge

# Winter

**W** inter is very cold and snowy
**I** ce is blue and very icy
**N** aughty people throw snowballs at people
**T** ell people to get ready for snow
**E** at all the food and snacks you want
**R** eady to get my warm hot chocolate.

**Jessica Bell (9)**
Antonine Primary School, Bonnybridge

# Winter

**W** hat a winter day at school
**I** went to the park
**N** ow it is snowing
**T** ired from playing in the snow all day
**E** veryone is playing with snowballs
**R** unning in the sparkling snow.

**Lucy Noble (9)**
Antonine Primary School, Bonnybridge

# Winter

**W** indy, freezing winter's day
**I** cy icicles under bridges
**N** athan and friend playing outside
**T** hey are having a snowball fight
**E** veryone is cold
**R** eady for Christmas.

**Xander Cameron (8)**
Antonine Primary School, Bonnybridge

# Winter

**W** inter is freezing every single day
**I** cy day at Christmas
**N** ight-time on Christmas
**T** ime to open presents
**E** very single day it's snowing
**R** aining on Christmas Day!

**Cameron Gibson (9)**
Antonine Primary School, Bonnybridge

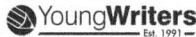

# Winter

**W** et white snow
**I** ce everywhere
**N** ice and cold
**T** he hot chocolate on the table
**E** very day my big garden is full of white snow
**R** olling the big soft blanket.

**Hamza Riaz (9)**
Antonine Primary School, Bonnybridge

# Chocolate And Cherries

*Haiku poetry*

You get it in bars
You get it in fridges, yum!
It is good to eat.

I found some cherries
And then I washed some cherries
Then I ate cherries.

**Sienna Kay (9)**
Antonine Primary School, Bonnybridge

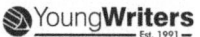

# Sweet, Sweet Birds

*A haiku*

Snow birds in the sky
Birds tweeting in the cold snow
Birds rolling in mud.

**Aaron Pittendreigh (9)**
Antonine Primary School, Bonnybridge

# The Big Christmas Tree

*A haiku*

The big Christmas tree
Was covered in lots of lights
That were very bright.

**Kai Blain (9)**
Antonine Primary School, Bonnybridge

# Not A Normal School Day

*A haiku*

As I see the school
Snow is falling around now
The leaves are pure white.

**Kian Stevenson (9)**
Antonine Primary School, Bonnybridge

# Takis

*A haiku*

They are so spicy
They are so crunchy and good
They are the best crisps.

**Madison Corrigan (9)**
Antonine Primary School, Bonnybridge

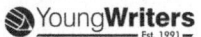

# The Little Robin
*A haiku*

The little robin
Was watching the snow fall down
Onto the cold ground.

**Kenzie Piper Wright (9)**
Antonine Primary School, Bonnybridge

# Icy Ice Spice

*A haiku*

Fresh air in the air
Car zooming on icy grass
Ice spice was frosty.

**Amy Callaghan (9)**
Antonine Primary School, Bonnybridge

# Bold Snow

*A haiku*

Kids in bed with hope
Snow is cold and icy bold
Cocoa in my hands.

**Halle Cunningham (9)**
Antonine Primary School, Bonnybridge

# Sweet Snow

*A haiku*

I love falling snow
I saw a snowy hedgehog
I like Christmas Day.

**Callan Logan (9)**
Antonine Primary School, Bonnybridge

# Spider

*A haiku*

Little spider wow
Your tiny body is weird
Like your life spider.

**Noah Charleston (9)**
Antonine Primary School, Bonnybridge

# Tiny Robin

*A haiku*

Tiny robin in
The cold in the snowy day
Don't be sad robin.

**Lucy Byars (9)**
Antonine Primary School, Bonnybridge

# Sweet Little Robin

*A haiku*

I saw a robin
In the tree chirping all day
The robin is small.

**Skye-Leigh Price (9)**
Antonine Primary School, Bonnybridge

# Survivors And I

The walkers are gone, not getting long,
Better start running, the master clock won't dong.
Walkers are back, better attack,
Ran over a branch and it went crack.

I found survivors, they're still alive,
They aren't insured, we'd better survive,
We found a car, it's new,
Then I found a stack of Mountain Dew.

A huge group came, now we have to be stealthy,
The huge group came, most food isn't healthy,
We found a gun, let's have some fun,
We took a turret, it weighs a tonne.

Most walkers are gone, let's have a blast,
Not many left, it's close to the last,
We're almost out, let's be fast,
We're out of food, we found a fishing rod, let's cast.

We're alive, it's finally over, yes, we are safe.

**Brandon Kennedy (10)**
Armoy Primary School, Ballymoney

# A Winter Wonderland

It's upside down in Dreamland.
The sky is as green as an emerald.
The floor is covered in clouds,
And birds chirp at our feet.

I opened my eyes, but was still asleep,
So quiet you couldn't hear a peep.
I looked around, nothing to see,
But a glimmering light beyond my feet.

I crept out of bed, legs like jelly, the floorboards creaked.
Soon, I realise it was my old wardrobe, as white as bleach.
I slowly opened the door and heard someone speak.
Scared, I let out a slight scream!

I opened the door as slowly as a snail; then the door creaked.
The blue eyes looked at me, his eyes as blue as the sea.
It came toward me as slow as can be.
Said, "Hi!" then I realised, he was half goat.

He talked to me and said, "Do you want to come with me for tea?"
So I agreed, walking through the crunchy leaves
And snow as loud as could be.

We arrived at his cottage for tea.
The cottage made of twigs from a tree.
He popped off the milk cap and we enjoyed our tea in peace.

## Charlotte Rainey (11)
Armoy Primary School, Ballymoney

# Around The World!

**N** orway is first, let's go to it! I see a goat! *Bahh!* Goat says, "Hi, wait, what?!"
**I** reland is next. "Hi, mate! What are you doing? Eating candy? Yummy!"
**G** uten tag! We are in Germany and there are flying cows! *Mooo!*
**H** ola! We're in Spain! Enjoy the heat, but, man, there are so many pigs talking!
**T** urkey! The ice cream man is tricking you! Haha!
**M** exico! There are flying tacos everywhere. *Bang!* Oh no, they're crushed! Arghh!
**A** merica is next! We're here! And there are cowboys and cowboys flying on cows!
**R** omania! My mum used to live there! But I still can't catch that magic chicken.
**E** gypt, finally! We're at the River Nile. Argh! A crocodile! Run!

**Sorana McCook (10)**
Armoy Primary School, Ballymoney

# My Liverpool Dream

Liverpool, the mighty Reds,
Having fun and making friends.
We're fielding such a strong defence,
They are through on goal, who finds the back of the net.

It's half-time break, I'm having a blast,
Loving life, the stadium's class.
Salah running down the wing very fast,
Chelsea players are getting mad at the fans.

Chelsea fans are leaving in dread,
But we're still cheering on the men in red.
At the minute, the Reds are having fun,
The scoreline is still six to none.

Big Konaté and Klopp signed my ball,
Then Klopp had a bit of a fall.
We all then sang, "You'll never walk alone."
The best club in the world they have shown.

**Jamie Simpson (10)**
Armoy Primary School, Ballymoney

# Shrek, The Green Ogre

It's upside down in Dreamland,
The sky is as green as an emerald,
The floor is covered in clouds,
And birds cheep at our feet,

I was at home when an ogre with an emerald,
Disturbed me making my mum a sapphire,
I got dragged into a world full of sea,
I fell in a lake as deep as can be,

But this soul helped me,
I was sitting confused when a wee guy came to me,
It was Donkey,
He was very silly,

He took me to a guy called Shrek,
I heard a bang as the door was wrecked,
Then a green guy came to me,
As quiet as can be,
He said he was Shrek
Shrek sat on a deck
Then me and him became friends
A friendship that will never end.

**Gracie Adams (10)**
Armoy Primary School, Ballymoney

# A Dream Come True

It's upside down in Dreamland,
The sky is as green as an emerald.
The floor is covered in clouds
And birds cheep at our feet,
It's a dream come true.

The majestic animals as loud as a band,
Playing guitars, violins and even drums too,
The sky is blue,
There are monkeys drinking Irn-Bru,
And there are giant marshmallows
That begin to move.

The chocolate is so bright I can't
Stand not taking a bite,
Then there is a crunch
That sounds like something I would munch.

The chocolate looks so nice.
I decide to take a bite,
Then Magicland turns into a messed-up zoo,
And that is the end of my dream come true.

**Sara Cushnahan (11)**
Armoy Primary School, Ballymoney

# The Candyland Dream

It's upside down in Dreamland and the sky is emerald-green
The floor is covered in clouds, and birds chirp at our feet
I saw a magic door, I walked right through it
I saw lots of sweets, candyfloss and sheep.

I saw a house made of chocolate brick with a candy cane roof
I found out the chocolate was waterproof.

I'm starting to get hungry, so I want to eat
I think I'm starting to miss meat.

I think I've eaten too much candy and I have to tell the truth
I think I'm starting to lose a tooth.

I turn around and I see
A talking candyfloss tree
I see a buzzing bee as yellow as the sun
Candyland dream is so much fun.

**Josh McCurdy (10)**
Armoy Primary School, Ballymoney

# Going To Bed With Ted

It's upside down in Dreamland,
The sky is as green as an emerald.
The floor is covered in clouds,
And birds cheep at our feet.

One night, I was getting ready to go to be with my Ted,
Ted hates going to bed, but I really love my bed!
My bed is so comfy, cosy, and soft.
When we got our beds, we fought!

My mum had to choose who got what,
Of course, she gave me the best one.
And I love it a tonne!
Then we brushed our teeth.

I like the noise that my bristles make,
Ted brushes his teeth, so fake.
Then we went into our rooms and we got our pyjamas.
Oh, my pyjamas, I have lovely llamas.

Goodnight!

**Emily Knox (10)**
Armoy Primary School, Ballymoney

# Dragon World

It's upside down in Dreamworld,
The sky is as green as an emerald,
The floor is covered in clouds,
And birds cheep at our feet,

*Whoosh, zoom, wheee,*
Hehe, what a race,
Lucky it wasn't a disgrace,
What a practice race,

Ally with his dark purple and green dragon,
That is insane,
Mine is blue and yellow, hit the wall,
At least it's not in pain,

Birds talking,
People walking,
Commentators rocking,

Flying two times the speed of a bird,
Listening to Mockingbird,
Flying along,
Listening to my favourite song,

See the finish,
All I have to do is go through to not vanish.

**Tyler Lyons (11)**
Armoy Primary School, Ballymoney

# Candy Land

**D** ragons flying in the blue sky, goblins dancing in the candy grass. Shrek in his candy swamp and magical creatures.
**R** oaming all around in the fields, cartoons having a good time. I see everything all around. I dance with glee, everyone is happy!
**E** nclosing me to see Shrek in a swamp so I run to see Shrek in person. I make it just in time to see the man.
**A** nxiety gets to me but it goes away very quickly. I have a conversation with Shrek; we become friends very quickly.
**M** ake tea as the sun starts to set. A dragon lies me on its back and *zooms!* The dragon takes me off. I feel excited!
**S** woosh through the Milky Way!

**Katie Boyle**
Armoy Primary School, Ballymoney

# My Nosy Nana

It's upside down in Dreamland,
The sky is as green as an emerald.
The floor is covered in clouds,
And birds cheep at our feet.
My nosy nana slipped on a banana,
Then she wore a bright blue bandana.

For supper, we had beans on toast.
I'm not trying to boast!
I just can't wait for ice cream.
I'm so happy, I could walk on a beam!

Now, we are playing 'Ludo'.
Then we will play a game of 'Cluedo'.
It's over now and I won,
Now I might go for a run.

I played with my dog,
He found a massive log.
Nana and I watched a movie.
It was actually quite groovy!

**Callie McCooke (9)**
Armoy Primary School, Ballymoney

# Bigfoot

It's upside down in Dreamland,
The sky is green as an emerald,
The floor is covered in clouds
And the birds cheep at our feet.

Deep in the forest lies a creature,
Big and hairy with a scary feature,
If you hear a crunch of leaves,
You'd better climb a dancing tree,
Call for help,
Let out a yelp!

In the forest, he will be snoring,
So you'd better not be roaring,
He will be hunting for food,
So you'd better not be rude.

If you snap a twig,
You'd better get out in a jig,
For the beast will hunt you fast,
And soon your life will be in the past.

**Archie McNeill (10)**
Armoy Primary School, Ballymoney

# The Death Of Me

It's upside down in Dreamland,
The sky is green,
The floor is covered in clouds,
And birds cheep at our feet.

Walking upon the beach,
The sea as blue as bleach.
The waves come in,
I'm under the sea's skin.

As I'm dragged under,
I see my life coming to a plunder.
I'm surely alone,
No one at all, I'm not wanting to moan.

The sea as dark as can be,
I see my eyes close slowly but surely.
As I'm slowly dragged under,
I realise my life was a blunder.

I am visualising what's going to be,
'The Death Of Me'.

**Riley Linton (11)**
Armoy Primary School, Ballymoney

# Footballer

Along the fields of Anfield Road, the fans were loud.
With clapping and chanting around the road of Anfield.

Fans chanting, clapping and cheering.
The footballers were hearing songs.
Liverpool FC is in the Champions League
And fans are going wild.

I thought I saw a goat on the boat.
Liverpool had a goat.
The referee on the pitch was called Matt.
Mohammed Salah kicks the ball with his left foot.

Alisson Becker is the world's best keeper.
Mo Salah is a right-winger.
Diogo Jota is a centre-forward.
Jürgen Klopp ordered.

**Noah Christie (10)**
Armoy Primary School, Ballymoney

# The Magical World Of Books

It's time to dream...
When I start dreaming, my house is beautiful and clean.
I walk over to my books and see every book you could ever think of!
What a dream!

I select a book.
It is about a pirate with a dangerous, scary hook.
I was a poor, horrible slave who stole some food.

Now it's time for a fairy tale.
I helped Rapunzel with her as soft as silk land.
Yes, she still lived to tell the tale!

Finally, it's time for our final story.
I'm Veruca Salt and I just went down the rubbish chute.
What a funny story!

**Grace Dobbin (10)**
Armoy Primary School, Ballymoney

# The Magic Book

It's upside down in Dreamland,
The sky is as green as an emerald,
The floor is covered in clouds,
And birds cheep at our feet,
But now I need something to eat,

I went to get some bread and butter,
And then I started to mutter,
I'm going to go to the library now,
I look in and think, *how?*

All the books have fell,
I'm going to go and tell,
I think they are over there,
But I don't know where!

I turned around and looked,
Then I saw a sparkling book!
I went right to it and opened it wide,
And found myself inside!

A magical amazing wonderland,
If you want to go just take my hand!

**Amelia Moore (9)**
Armoy Primary School, Ballymoney

# Untitled

David Willams and I were mates,
Then David said, "What if a tree was on a date?"
Then I said, "Let's steal something from Doctor Who before it's too late."

We were in the lab and I was glad,
Then I saw the time machine and David was mad.
Then David said to me that I was bad.

The police showed up and we were sad,
And that was that we were too bad.
The policeman was glad.

David and I were mad,
Then we found a strange granny, then we found Danny.
We got released, then we had a cup of tea.

**Owen Boyle (11)**
Armoy Primary School, Ballymoney

# My Fantastic Firework Night

It's upside down in Dreamland,
The sky is as green as an emerald.
The floor is covered in clouds,
And birds cheep at our feet.

At night, I love the clashing fireworks,
The pop and sound of bashing.

I'm out with my friends,
And we're having a great time.
How long will it last?
We're all having a blast time.
We don't want the fun to stop.

It's time for the fireworks display,
And we're all excited.
It's my birthday, so we are out partying.
The fun will never stop.

**Jessica Leeming (10)**
Armoy Primary School, Ballymoney

# The Golden Eye

A young boy, about 10 or 11.
As he walked through the clouds, it felt like Heaven.
But then he saw a small golden eye,
And as he did he began to fly.
He flew and flew into a huge grey cave.
I could have said he was fearless, but he was not so brave.

He ran the cave up and down,
But then he began to frown.
He ran and ran all the way back.
He found a sack pushed into the ground.
But now he lies in his bed safe and sound.
Now he is in his tiny little bed,
And the golden eye was all in his head.

**Oliver McCook (11)**
Armoy Primary School, Ballymoney

# Teletubbies Scared

All good in Teletubbyland
The Teletubbies are making a band
The next day the Teletubbies heard an ultrasound
It seemed it was an animal making a sound.

The Teletubbies knew what they heard
The telly was very scared
There was a bee as stingy as a nettle chasing them
There was a crash
Po fell, now she has a rash.

The Teletubbies jumped in a pool of custard
Then the Teletubbies washed their hair with mustard
The Teletubbies had a bottle of Prime
Then it was Teletubby bedtime.

**Molly Moore**
Armoy Primary School, Ballymoney

# My Dream Job

**N** ew cows arriving, mooing.
**I** have a John Deere tractor, it is being driven by a chicken.
**G** reen grass is being cut by a mower zooming.
**H** ave a sheepdog to help me get the sheep in.
**T** wo 7530s arriving in my yard, hurrying I went.
**M** y chicken went into my jeep and tried to drive the jeep.
**A** rushing milk lorry arrives to get the milk.
**R** eversing the John Deere tractor.
**E** verybody was getting ready for silage and I was getting ready too.

**Mason Kane (9)**
Armoy Primary School, Ballymoney

# Road To The Final

As nervous as it can be from start to end,
It can start to bend,
From group stage to the final,
It can be vital.

The commentators crunching
It could be munchy.
They kicked off with a whistle
But it might be a missile.

One-nil up
We might win the cup!
Two-nil up; this man is guff!
From Best to Diego, it might be rough.

Three-nil up,
We will win the group.
The final whistle
It was like playing tinsel.

**Danny Mooney (11)**
Armoy Primary School, Ballymoney

# My Washing Came Alive

**N** ever in my life have I seen this before.
**I** thought I saw the clothes move.
**G** ive them a massive kick to make them move.
"**H** ave I done something to you?" said the clothes.
**T** he clothes start to dance and prance.
**M** anic, the house goes mad.
**A** nd the clothes run down the street.
**R** un, run, he stops and does a blackflip.
**E** nd of the night, I finally woke.

**Carson Irvine (10)**
Armoy Primary School, Ballymoney

# The Iron Boy

*Clink! Clink! Clonk!* went my hammer.
I'm building the Iron Boy,
He will not be a toy.
It took me two weeks to build.

It was filled with wires and microchips
And all the other bits.
The steel was as cold as snow,
And he was very slow.

I was walking around with him
And then we thought we saw another version of him.
Finally, it was time to go
Back to our home.

**Noah Johnston (10)**
Armoy Primary School, Ballymoney

# Untitled

**D** reaming in the fields is so much fun with the horses.
**R** ory is the stable cat and Max is the stable dog. They are adorable.
**E** very day riding horses and I can see the sun smiling down.
**A** mazing my friends came and we were racing and having fun.
**M** y horses are called Poppy and Rokey but my mum came and picked me up.
**S** o tomorrow I'm going back to the stable.

**Lexi O'Lone (9)**
Armoy Primary School, Ballymoney

# Nightmare On The Farm

**N** ew Case Puma 265 was moving very loudly.
**I** n the wellie boot, something moved.
**G** rass is being grazed by the cows.
**H** ens fly through the sky.
**T** wo sheep, "Baa," when going to the market.
**M** y jeep sounds like a tractor.
**A** John Deere's very noisy.
**R** ear mower 70ft.
**E** ven a tractor with wings.

**William Hanna (10)**
Armoy Primary School, Ballymoney

# Taylor Swift

**D** reaming about going to a Taylor Swift concert is one of my biggest dreams.
**R** iding in the car singing Taylor Swift songs.
**E** ating before the concert, so I don't go hungry.
**A** m so excited to see Taylor Swift.
**M** y favourite song came on, and I sang my heart out.
**S** he dances like a professional dancer.

**Macy Elder (10)**
Armoy Primary School, Ballymoney

# Squishmallow Land

As I lay in my bed
An amazing dream came into my head
Squishmallow Land, a beautiful place
Millions of Squishmallows playing with grace.

Marshmallow toadstools
And candyfloss clouds everywhere
Yet all the Squishmallows
Were so unaware.

Wicked Queen Delphine was up in her castle
Trying to make a lot of hassle
Cherry blossom, lavender, peach and pastel-blue
Can you see all the pretty colours? 'Cause I do!

Delphine, the wicked queen, wanted everything grey
She didn't want the Squishmallows to be able to play
A magic vacuum she has under her bed
Although the instructions she hadn't quite read.

She pushed the button
Hoping to suck all the colour away
She let out a squeal
When the colours weren't grey.

Instead
The colours got more intense
Queen Delphine
Didn't think it made sense.

She appreciated
All these bright new colours
And started playing
With the others.

Squishmallow Land
Was brighter than ever before
When I woke up
I wanted to dream more...

**Evie Truesdale (8)**
Braidside Integrated Primary And Nursery School, Ballymena

# No Dreams, Just Nightmares

When I go to bed at night,
I hope to have some dreams.
But fairies, flowers and fields of green,
Are nowhere to be seen.

When I close my eyes at night and fall asleep,
Instead, I see a darkness and hear things that creep.
There are trees throughout that seem to be burnt,
But behind the trees, I hear laughter from her.

I see a shadow from behind the tree.
It looks like a person.
Then I see a head; it looks creepy!

Suddenly, I feel a tap on my shoulder.
I turn around; it is a clown.
It starts to chase me!

Suddenly, it disappears.
Then I see my worst fear; spiders as big as a dog!
Then something grabs me, I tremble with fear.
It drops me. It is a monster.
I run, more monsters appear.
I run faster and faster and faster!

They start to run, I trip over a twig.
I wake up with a scream!
My mum and dad come to check on me.
I say it's all okay, it was just a dream.

### Lila Dunceith (8)
Braidside Integrated Primary And Nursery School, Ballymena

# Hot Chocolate Land

Chocolate, chocolate, everywhere
But not a drop to drink.
If he can convince you to take a sip
Then you shall surely sink.

What looks like birds fly in the air
But not a chirp anywhere.
Marshmallow birds they seem to be
What a strange sight to see.
They float so high
But when it's hot they melt and die.

My chocolate dog is so sweet
Running with me at my feet.
Max is my friend, so strong and brave
With me through this chocolate craze.

The monster makes it smell so sweet
But if you taste it, then none shall meet.
My friend and I we run to hide
To our house, where none shall find.

With chocolate walls that smell so sweet
This chocolate here we can surely eat.
Safe and warm where no monster can find
We shall stay here within our mind.

**Emilie Barr (9)**
Braidside Integrated Primary And Nursery School, Ballymena

# The Dream Flower

Once upon a dream,
Things weren't as they seemed.
There's a land inside your head.
When dreams aren't made, they're grown.

On a flower so vast it would make you gasp.
Stems stretch out left and right,
With bubbles at the end, full of delight.
But if the stems grow past the barrier,
It's into nightmares, full of disaster.

Once the dream master checks the dreams,
They're sent to play in your head.
Sweet dreams!
But if the dreams stretched past the barrier,
The Nightmare King checks it.

A night full of disaster!

**Shannon Payne (9)**
Braidside Integrated Primary And Nursery School, Ballymena

# Miracle Island

I live on an island
Surrounding by trees,
They are yellow in colour
With big blue leaves.

I built my house
With wood and stone,
And my best friend
Is a winged lion named Bone.

My magical garden
Is filled with creatures,
With weird and wonderful
Unusual features.

A lion with wings
An elephant pig,
And a giant sloth
Wearing a wig!

These are just some of the creatures
Living with me,
And I am just happy
As can be!

**Tommy Swann (9)**
Braidside Integrated Primary And Nursery School, Ballymena

# Football

**F** abulous kick as it goes into the net and makes the first goal.
**O** utstanding team. The parents whisper, "That team is amazing."
**O** vercome your fear to play on a field with lots of people watching.
**T** errific goalkeeper as he nearly saves all the shots.
**B** rilliant ball with its super speed, flying across the field.
**A** wesome and active players all around the field.
**L** ively players with lots of energy.
**L** oyal to be on the field.

### Emilie Thompson (9)
Braidside Integrated Primary And Nursery School, Ballymena

# If Stitch Was Real

If Stitch was real,
I would make him this deal.
I would show him exactly
How I would feel.

I would give him some ink,
And let him colour me pink
And take him to school,
To see what my friends would think.

We would laugh and play
Throughout the day,
I can only imagine
What everyone would say.

If Stitch was real
That would be the deal.
I would be his best friend, Angel
And proud is how I would feel.

**Liberty Stewart (9)**
Braidside Integrated Primary And Nursery School, Ballymena

# Footballer

**F** illed with happiness as we score
**O** h hi, I want to be the next Mo Salah
**O** ut of all the other clubs, I chose Liverpool
**T** he ball came to me and I scored
**"B** elieve in your dreams," they said
**A** t the match, I met Mo Salah
**L** oving football right now
**L** iverpool is not just a team
**E** verywhere we go, people want to know
**R** aging because we lost the match.

**Preston Balmer (9)**
Braidside Integrated Primary And Nursery School, Ballymena

# Love And Happiness

Imagination is free,
In my world of dreams.
Where everyone is happy,
And love is there for me.

My mum and dad,
At the end of the rainbow,
My brothers and sister,
I see their hearts glow.

Up in the clouds,
We all float around.
I feel so safe,
I wish this were real.

Imagination is free,
In my world of dreams,
Of rainbows and unicorns,
And whatever you want to be.

**Hallie-Mae Quigley (8)**
Braidside Integrated Primary And Nursery School, Ballymena

# Above The Clouds

I close my eyes and go to sleep
Until the morning, I'll not peep.
Off to a land with dragons and fairies
A land of dreams where there are no scaries.

A house floating gracefully on a cloud,
I meet my cousin, Hannah and feel so proud.
Together we are united and ready to explore
But the time flies in and we want to see more.

Then I hear that familiar beep
Alexa, turn off. I want to sleep!

**Annie Corry (8)**
Braidside Integrated Primary And Nursery School, Ballymena

# The Life Of A Footballer

**F** antastic skills they all have,
**O** ver 300 goals to be scored,
**O** ther players can get bored.
**T** he atmosphere is unread
**B** ecause of the crowd's cheers.
**A** nywhere in the world, football can be played.
**L** ife can change with the kick of a ball.
**L** eaving the stadium makes me feel so good that only my dad and I can understand.

**Darcie Williamsam (8)**
Braidside Integrated Primary And Nursery School, Ballymena

# Math Dogs

**M** ath dogs sit in teachers' chairs.
**A** ll of them have funny hair.
**T** hrough the window, I can see.
**H** appy dogs with cups of tea.

**D** o you really need to shout?
**O** ne math dog says, "Please don't pout."
**G** o and have a sit on the chair.
**S** o it is nearly my turn now, then I'm sleeping with mad hair.

**Erin Nelson (9)**
Braidside Integrated Primary And Nursery School, Ballymena

# Minecraft Dreaming

**M** y dream is to live in Minecraft.
**I** live in a world where
**N** othing is as it seems.
**E** ndermen are corrupt players,
**C** reepers are afraid of cats.
**R** avagers are large, hostile mobs,
**A** ttacking players and traders.
**F** arland can still be found as bedrock.
**T** his could be my Dreamland in Magical Mystery World.

**Reuben Dinsmore (9)**
Braidside Integrated Primary And Nursery School, Ballymena

# Footprints In The Snow

I snuggled up in bed last night,
And drifted off to sleep.
Suddenly, there was Lila wearing
A hat, scarf and fluffy gloves.

Off we went on a snowy walk,
And saw footprints in the snow.
Big ones, little ones,
Small ones, cat ones,
Bird ones, dog ones,
And pretty little baby ones.

**Sophia Elliott (9)**
Braidside Integrated Primary And Nursery School, Ballymena

# Super Star

Once upon a shooting star,
I wished to become a 'Super Star'.
I dreamt of fancy clothes, plenty of style,
And hoped it would last for more than a while.

I love to dress and impress
And make plenty of mess!
I hope one day to get plenty of pay
And this would make me smile all day.

**Erin Rose (8)**
Braidside Integrated Primary And Nursery School, Ballymena

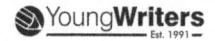

# Rainbow Clouds

I am dreaming of being in the big, fluffy clouds and singing out loud,
Standing very proud
Wearing my beautiful, bright surround dress,
Oh how wonderful it would be for me
Bowing in front of a big crowd
Up in a big, colourful rainbow cloud.

**Sophia McNeill (9)**
Braidside Integrated Primary And Nursery School, Ballymena

# The Wolves' Kingdom

A dark place is where I be,
Under full moonlight is where I see.
Wolves rushing here and there,
Chasing something small and scared.
This tiny shadow had pricked-up ears.
It hid in a log with great fears.

I slowly approached, making no noise.
As the tiny shadow spoke, I heard a squeaky voice.
"Help me! Help me! I'm being chased by wolves.
If only you could stop them or make them duel!"

Accepting the plea, the tiny bunny I touched,
And with a flare and a flicker,
We flew away in stardust.

**Ella Prouton (9)**
Charlton House School, Bitterne Park

# Never Have I Seen

Never have I seen
Such a lovely but horrible dream.

I was at home
With my cat, Knome,
I clapped my hands and whistled twice
And a portal appeared with something nice.

My other cat, Brice
Looked at me with a bucket of ice,
The place was covered with smoke
Don't ask me if you think it's a joke.

I ran when I saw the place on fire
With a man named Sire,
I tried to help
But the man started to yelp.

I whistled twice
And threw the bucket of ice,
That I got from Brice.

I told Sire never to hunt the golden leaves
Or you are going to have fifty cats on your sleeve.

So I waved goodbye, and off I go
So I could not smell the scent, you know.

I closed my eyes and jumped into the portal
So that I didn't become immortal.

I found my sweet cousin, Ed
Sitting on my bed.

I woke up and realised it was a dream
That I had never seen.

**Keyara Minors (10)**
Charlton House School, Bitterne Park

# The Magical Forest

It's so natural
Has butterflies around
Also has magical creatures
Always has fairies around
And sometimes the baddies are around
And fairies don't like it when the baddies are around
The ladybird likes to crawl around
I hope I can fly from the ground so we can play
A twinkle from the star and it will be granted.

**Ayesha Iqbal (10)**
Charlton House School, Bitterne Park

# Bricks

**B** locks in a dream, I usually have,
**R** ed ones made of stone,
**I** n a land far from home,
**C** racks you will never see in them,
**K** itten Tower is what I make,
**S** o I am happy in bed every night.

**Oliver Noble (10)**
Charlton House School, Bitterne Park

# Prides

I met a lioness,
And they were happy to see me.
Simba was the youngest lion.
His dad was called Mufasa.

His brother was called Scar.
Scar tried to kick me.
Mustafa said, "Stop, Scar!"
Scar looked after Simba.

Simba grew to be a big lion
When Mufasa had died.
But I have to be in charge of the lioness.

Simba called Nala, the girl lion.
She was the helper for the rest of the lionesses.

**Ari Feldmann (9)**
Gesher School, Pinner

# My Poem

My dream is to be a YouTube star
I will be famous near and far
My videos will be about the tube and train
My followers will watch them again and again
Suddenly, I reached a thousand subscribers and I was glad!
Everyone was proud, even Mum and Dad
We had a party to celebrate and ate lots of cake
With all my friends including Jake
And surprisingly I reached one million subscribers!
I can't believe I have that many admirers.

**Leon Krett (9)**
Gesher School, Pinner

# The Pokémon Dream

I go to bed by my dad and mum
But, if I was going to act my age, I had to sleep on my own
I dream about a world where Pokémon are my best friends
We could play and I could train them and battle with them
And also have adventures together
But then it was morning
My mum woke me up and said,
"Good morning!"
I was confused,
"Mum, why are you waking me up so early?"

**Advait Raipara (9)**
Gesher School, Pinner

# The Magical Unicorn

I was on the Easy Jet
And I really missed my pet.
I started to skydive
So I could be alive.

I saw a unicorn
And it had a shiny horn.
Then I flew on its back
And it sang me a rap.

**Poppy Hass (8)**
Gesher School, Pinner

# The Flying Monsters

**T** he monsters flying in the sky.
**H** aving fun way up high.
**E** very monster is so big.

**F** airies hiding in the twigs.
**L** aughing, dancing, having fun.
**Y** awning, so dumb, the monsters are near them.
**I** see flying monsters above my head.
**N** ever again will I dream of flying monsters being mean.
**G** iant monsters, scary and hairy.

**M** agical and flying fairies scared of the hairies
**O** ver the dirty waves
**N** othing is going to stop us finding the shiny gold
**S** uddenly it was dark and gloomy
**T** rying to sleep but the sound of waves is too loud
**E** very night is my dream
**R** emembering not to scream
**S** illy monsters don't scare me anymore.

### Connie Lee (10)
Glyncorrwg Primary School, Glyncorrwg

# The Night Wizards

**N** ight wizards try to fight on a dark gloomy night.
**I** see a dark figure walking ready to fight.
**G** o away I say, but they can't hear me, I am too quiet.
**H** elp! Help! I scream but no one is here.
**T** he night wizards come very close to me but I disappear.

**W** here am I now, I think I'm in the castle.
**I** see another one but I have got power.
**Z** ombie I scream to scare the wizards... Arghh they scream.
**A** nything can be magic if you dream it.
**R** ight I say let's explore... Arghh, a real zombie, please explode.
**D** reaming is a magical thing I say.

**Gracie Quinn (9)**
Glyncorrwg Primary School, Glyncorrwg

# Royal Football

**R** ashford scoring goals.
**O** nana can't save Rashford's mighty goals.
**Y** ellow cards make the game extremely hard.
**A** lways a big fan of the game.
**L** oud crowd, fans are super proud.

**F** ootball is the best game ever.
**O** ur Hotspur son never misses.
**O** ur hearts are full of pride.
**T** ime to play, no more misses.
**B** etter than any team.
**A** ll young players make the dream.
**L** oyal footballers on the pitch.
**L** ovely fans trying to get rich.

**Zak Williams (10)**
Glyncorrwg Primary School, Glyncorrwg

# Queens Palace

**Q** ueen's palace shines bottom to top!
**U** nique it shines off the light it pops
**E** merald, rubies and diamonds all around
**E** very brick is silver and gold.
**N** ew invites get delivered every day
**S** afely to my door for my say.

**P** arties are magical fun, fun, fun!
**A** rtworks are finally done
**L** egendary rooms are full of kings
**A** ncient hands are covered with rings
**C** rowns are everywhere
**E** ven in the palace for all to care.

**Lucy Protheroe (10)**
Glyncorrwg Primary School, Glyncorrwg

# Galloping Horses

**H** orses galloping all around. All my friends pulling the reins to slow them down.
**O** ver the green fields, they go galloping along, with the strong wind hitting their face.
**R** acing all over the big green fields, trying to keep up with their pace.
**S** o many stables and horses at the farm, I can't count because it's too far.
**E** questrians don't mess around, they help the horses to keep them standing on the ground.
**S** o thrilled and happy to be on this hack with my friends.

**Isabel Lloyd (8)**
Glyncorrwg Primary School, Glyncorrwg

# The Jump-Scare

In my dream I hear a thud,
Spiders crawling up above,
My door opens, I close my eyes,
I open my eyes with a big fright,
There stands a big hairy monster,
Glowing, prowling with a cluster.
I try to scream but no noise seems to be,
I look out my window and there are monsters, clowns and grizzly bears too,
Bashing my door saying, "Boo!"
I open my eyes in real life,
I am safe at home tricked by my mind.

**Marnie Dennedy-Doyle (9)**
Glyncorrwg Primary School, Glyncorrwg

# My Fast Motorbike

**M** ountains bumpy, green and brown
**O** n my motorbike driving upside down
**T** rees are swaying in the breeze
**O** ut jumps my dad, I freeze
**R** evving the engine, I go slow
"**B** rake Dad!" Down he goes
**I** see blood dripping down his leg
**K** icking out he starts to beg
**E** veryone sees his head like an egg
**S** adly Dad won't go on my motorbike again!

**Albie Williams (8)**
Glyncorrwg Primary School, Glyncorrwg

# Doctor Who

**D** aleks attacking the world
**O** ne by one flying down to Earth
**C** oming down in a blue police box
**T** he big blue box has a man inside
**O** utside in my backyard, *it crashed.*
**R** unning down the stairs I go.

**W** ho could it be coming out of the blue box?
**H** orrible Daleks go in my backyard
**O** ver us, the biggest spaceship is landing.

**Ollie Bufton (10)**
Glyncorrwg Primary School, Glyncorrwg

# The Jump-Scare!

**T** he wizards flying high in the sky
**H** aving way too much fun, trying to die
**E** nergetic pirates waiting for people to scare

**S** hadows gleaming towards me
**C** aptain Pirate shouting, "Jump-scare time!"
**A** bandoned haunted house to do the scare
**R** ocking and rumbling on the stairs
**E** xpanding the dancer's leg from the jump-scare.

**Olivia Enoch (10)**
Glyncorrwg Primary School, Glyncorrwg

# Monsters

**M** ean monsters go to the cafe for some breakfast
**O** n a wild night, the monsters scare the bears
**N** obody around in the monsters' cave
**S** caring people time after time
**T** ogether the monsters will scare people
**E** very monster is a different type
**R** unning monster is fast, the sporty monster is sporty
**S** caring the people in the cafe.

**Tabitha Meredith (9)**
Glyncorrwg Primary School, Glyncorrwg

# Heroes Versus Villains

**S** unny day, nice and calm,
**U** p on the rooftop, causing no harm.
**P** owers going everywhere.
**E** veryone amused.
**R** ound two of the battle.
**P** eople hiding in the distance in a daze.
**O** ver the field, I saw
**W** andering villains with mighty claws.
**E** veryone comes from hiding.
**R** ough suits torn and ripped apart.

**Lily White (11)**
Glyncorrwg Primary School, Glyncorrwg

# Cloud City

**C** loud, all white and fluffy,
**L** ike a cute white puppy.
**O** n a cloud, feels like cotton candy.
**U** p in the sky, I can fly!
**D** oves and robins in the sky,

Can I fly? I don't know.
I wake up. Oh! It was a dream.
The new day might be good.
Why did I wake up?!
I hate to be awake!

**Kayden Walters (10)**
Glyncorrwg Primary School, Glyncorrwg

# Football

**F** ootball field so big and wide,
**O** ff the ball they take a stride,
**O** ver the post the ball flies,
**T** ottenham Hotspurs always cry,
**B** ut I am a Hotspur till I die.
**A** ll the Tottenham team starts to realise,
**L** oud fans start to go wild,
**L** ove the game, at least they tried.

**Autumn-Fayy Jones (9)**
Glyncorrwg Primary School, Glyncorrwg

# The Royal Kingdom

**F** lying spiders in the air
**L** ying on the grass, I could see a massive castle within
**Y** oung royalty inside the royal kingdom
**I** saw a wizard going in the royal kingdom
**N** othing there except for a bunch of spiders and wizards
**G** rowing through the ground are a few tiny, little flowers.

**Jackson Warlow (11)**
Glyncorrwg Primary School, Glyncorrwg

# Sea Full Of Cats

I find myself in a sea full of cats.
Luckily they have got rid of all the rats.
I feel confused but they are not amused.
I see bats flying near the cats but still, I see no rats.
A tuna can boat comes by but sadly it turns into a fly.
I feel sad in the sea full of cats.
But luckily they got rid of all the rats.

**Levi Woodbridge (10)**
Glyncorrwg Primary School, Glyncorrwg

# Monkey Land

**M** y head was hurting when I woke up
**O** n a mystical place up above
**N** ow I noticed a silhouette
**K** new I'm up above, I'm in Heaven, I shouted out loud
**E** verybody was very short, I went to look and they were monkeys
**Y** oung monkeys to be exact, there were banana trees as well.

**Sonny-Rayy Jones (10)**
Glyncorrwg Primary School, Glyncorrwg

# The Enchanted Kingdom

I was walking through a forest,
I saw a pirate named Dores.
We walked through the tall trees,
We saw bumblebees.
We walked curious and excited,
Fairies danced, delighted.
We found a kingdom,
That had some wisdom.
As we explored nothing to be found
Except for a tiny little crown.

**Maigan Fields (10)**
Glyncorrwg Primary School, Glyncorrwg

# The Magic Fairy Land

**F** un fairies flying across the land
**A** mazing fairies start to sing in the sand
**I** n the magic world, the unicorns start to run
**R** ieva P and I riding on the colourful unicorns having fun
**Y** ellow moonbeams shining down upon the sky, shiny sun flashing in my eye.

**Roshi Garrity (9)**
Glyncorrwg Primary School, Glyncorrwg

# The Dancing Fairies

The dancing fairies fly so high
We go to UDC for fun
When I dance, I am the sun
Roshi, Celia and Lucy too
Every dance we follow it through
Everyone dancing, prancing too!
Marnie signing up to have fun too
Tracey said,
"Time to go, come back soon,
Hope to see you back through the door."

**Seren McCabe (9)**
Glyncorrwg Primary School, Glyncorrwg

# The Magic Monsters

**M** agic wizards flying all around.
**A** ll the witches chasing them down.
**G** ood and bad, who will win?
**I** n the forest, there are some monsters sleeping in the bin!
**C** areful not to wake them up or they will turn you into a cup.

**Lucy Bath (9)**
Glyncorrwg Primary School, Glyncorrwg

# Clowns

**C** lowns dancing in the sea
**L** aughing, prancing, following me
**O** n the seashore with my hyper-energy
**W** aves in the sea, so friendly
**N** ever go where they can see
**S** o hyper you can't believe.

**Craig Fullerton (9)**
Glyncorrwg Primary School, Glyncorrwg

# Magical Dreams

When my head hits the pillow, who knows where I go?
My mind begins to work; it starts to glow.
I no longer care about life on the ground,
Only words in my head that still haven't been found.

These magical things, dreams they are called,
After a day of hard work, they are like a reward.
Just letting me drift off into my imagination,
It's my own world that does this creation.

Will there be unicorns and candyfloss all lovely and sweet?
Will there be thrilling mysteries with danger at your feet?
Will it be a funny dream with dancing centipedes,
Or will it be about sorcerers with secret remedies?

Dreams have the power to make anything possible,
You can be a hero, and you can be unstoppable.
Save the seas and save the land,
Unite in peace and give the Earth a hand.

Some might say that dreams are just in your head,
But if you let them out and work quite hard,
Then maybe, just maybe, they can be real instead.

**Luciana Diaz-Jimenez (9)**
Holy Cross Preparatory School, Kingston Upon Thames

# Dreams

Night is a time for dreaming along,
Maybe it's about you singing a song,
You could be making your first friend,
Or you could be doing your very first backbend.

You might come top of the class like Hermione Granger,
But you might meet a stinky old stranger!
It might be a nightmare or a sweetie dream,
You could be swimming in a sugar stream!

Maybe you'll be great at history,
But you might solve a mystery,
You could have a pet cat,
Or a dog who always sits on a mat.

You could be drinking hot choc,
Or for Christmas you're allowed tick-tock,
Maybe you'll get £1,000,
Or you could hear strange sounds.

Lovely dreams you sleep in peace,
Bad dreams you always tease,
Now, rest your spine,
For it's dreaming time!

**Alice Le Broussois (10)**
Holy Cross Preparatory School, Kingston Upon Thames

# My Worst Nightmare

One cold winter's night,
I awoke wide awake and bright.
I climbed out of bed and what did I see,
But a trillion black, hairy spiders scuttling below me.

My heart paused, my blood ran cold,
A dozen snakes, curled on the banister, thick and old.
Evil eyes bored into my heart,
As I wondered how to depart.

Out of the door I dashed,
Out of the door, out of the door, out of the door I thrashed.
Into a wood, a deep, dark wood,
Where skeletal trees stood.

Out of a bush came a beast,
A beast who wanted a feast!
My eyes widened in fear,
As it began to nibble my ear!

As I felt my head fill with dread,
I woke up in my warm, cosy bed!
My eyes grew wide as I started to chatter,
And my mum came in to find out what was the matter!

**Olanna Nwafor (10)**
Holy Cross Preparatory School, Kingston Upon Thames

# Dreams

Dancing around in my mystical mind,
I don't really know what it seems to be,
But something I do know is what's happening inside,
Is slowly created are my magical dreams!

Dreams of dinosaurs, unicorns, thriller scenes,
The improbable, impossible, the reality,
Being the leader of all, the judge, the queen,
All fun, all chaos, all a catastrophe!

But the worst dream of all isn't even one,
A villain, a criminal in his evil lair,
There are no bunnies, no happiness, no fun,
The dream I truly hate the most is a horrible nightmare.

But not today I will have them,
I just wanna party and be me,
Glistening in the sun, a crystal gem,
All I'm going to have is a perfect dream.

**Vasundhara Bahree (9)**
Holy Cross Preparatory School, Kingston Upon Thames

# The Land Of The Impossible

Once upon a dream
In a land far away,
Where one magic touch, created glitter and gleam,
This fantasy world came alive right away.
Dinosaurs to dragons and pirates to pixies,
Giggles and laughter spread very quickly.

Soldiers were aligned and the food was divine,
As the witches chanted spells,
"Frogs and snake skin all around,
Mice and hedgehogs get ready to pound!"
Smoke vigorously encircled the land,
When all you could hear was the deafening band.

The animals soared through the air,
Elephants to monkeys and horses to bears,
Each gleefully representing a clue,
Nothing you wish for can come true:
Without a dream.

**Jasmin Patel (9)**
Holy Cross Preparatory School, Kingston Upon Thames

# I Had A Dream

I had a dream that me and my twin,
We went for a swim,
In an extraordinary lake,
So extraordinary that we thought it was fake.

I had a dream that I saw a unicorn,
It was white with a shiny horn,
I couldn't believe my eyes,
When I saw a fairy in disguise.

I had a dream that there were monsters out,
We were so scared that we had to shout,
They were like creepy-crawlies under the bed,
All I wanted was to get them out of my head.

I had a dream that the trees were looking at me,
The trees were looking at me so weirdly,
There were so many little spiders,
And today I feel like one of those little writers.

**Raya Al-Derzi (9)**
Holy Cross Preparatory School, Kingston Upon Thames

# The Unicorns Of The Night

Every night, in my bed,
I close my eyes and fill my head,
With thoughts of the most wondrous things,
Like unicorns with sparkly wings.

They soar above the clouds so high,
In the darkness of the sky,
While jealous stars dance and twirl,
For me, Amalia, the lucky girl.

Their velvet backs, their golden hooves,
Their super funky dancing moves,
Those unicorns are by far the best,
Even more marvellous than the rest.

We play until the time is done,
For me to have such lovely fun,
I say, "Goodbye," to the unicorn team,
And soon I wake up; it was all a dream!

**Amalia Vilaseco (9)**
Holy Cross Preparatory School, Kingston Upon Thames

# My Best Dinnermare

I sit down to eat my dinner,
Horrors spread out on my plate,
Cabbage, peas and beans,
How could this get worse? Did I really have to eat it?
Horrid ham and not super sausage!
How could I do it, how, how, how?
I sighed, and stuck out my tongue
I really, really didn't want to eat it!

My food, it had a mind of its own,
It jumped down the table,
Boing, boing, boing,
It ripped right through and began to dance,
I was jumping up and dancing around,
Nothing could be better,
I loved it, loved it, loved it!

Sadly I woke up with a start,
To find it was just a dream.

**Lara Chakravarty (9)**
Holy Cross Preparatory School, Kingston Upon Thames

# Dreaming Wonderland

As I lay in bed and closed my eyes;
Up in the sky, there was a surprise;
Glowing unicorns flew in the air;
Guess what was rainbow? It was its hair.

Next, I was riding on a huge cloud;
I was flying! I was super proud;
Until a dragon blew on my cloud;
It blew huge flames and it also growled.

*Whoosh!* I landed on somewhere quite soft;
Actually, it was softer than soft;
There was a horn, it shone in the sun.
It was the unicorn, the bright one.

"Wake up! It's 6am! Time for school!"
I woke up as I thought, *that was cool.*

**Sophia Kim (10)**
Holy Cross Preparatory School, Kingston Upon Thames

# All Day Long The Fight Went On

I once saw a dog so I gave it a pat on the back
But he never liked that
So I sang him a song
But he didn't follow along
He lay on his back
And cried for a reply back
And there came his dad storming right back
But then came out a black and white cat
Prancing onto the left path
And hissing just like a bat
All day long the fight went on
And just like that
The cat stopped hissing like a bat.

**Izabella Faith-Brown (10)**
**Northlew And Ashbury Primary Parochial CE School, Okehampton**

# Countdown

**C** ountless nights without sleep.
**O** verexcited just need a peep.
**U** nderstand why I'm scared.
**N** ow I'm lying here unprepared.
**T** wisting and turning alone in my bed.
**D** ark and quiet, this is what I dread.
**O** wning up to my fears.
**W** aking up.
**N** ow entering, I'm safe here.

Congratulations Mr and Mrs Sallow, you have a beautiful baby girl.

**Darcie Canham (10)**
Northlew And Ashbury Primary Parochial CE School, Okehampton

# Once I Had A Dream

Once I had a dream,
I saw a merry, little thing.
It was walking along a path.
It had a little laugh.
It beckoned to follow,
I went through a bush and I hit my head on a roof.
For there in front of me was a little house
And out came a little mouse.
It looked at me confused and puzzled without a doubt.
I don't blame it, I just bumped into its house.
What a weird dream I had.

**Arabella Porteous (10)**
Northlew And Ashbury Primary Parochial CE School, Okehampton

# Astronaut

**A** person braver than any I've seen,
**S** ilently drifting in a midnight dream.
**T** ogether with the stars at night,
**R** oaring through the galaxy is not a fright.
**O** ver the constellations,
**N** ow I see,
**A** purple sky
**U** pon me.
**T** wisting and turning, I wake up with a
**S** tart, and feel my chest, a pounding heart.

**Thea Page (10)**
Northlew And Ashbury Primary Parochial CE School, Okehampton

# Unicorns

**U** nique is a unicorn,
**N** o one has ever seen one though,
**I** n my dreams, they live upon a cloud,
**C** atcorns also live there,
**O** ver the hill and up a stair,
**R** un around, it's over there!
**N** ow we have found them, let's celebrate!
**S** uper night, that's what we've had, now let's awake for today.

**Laila Chastey (9)**
Northlew And Ashbury Primary Parochial CE School, Okehampton

# Untitled

**T** rying my best,
**R** especting other people's machines,
**A** pproaching a beautiful farm,
**C** limbing in a beautiful tractor's cab,
**T** rying to afford massive machines,
**O** n the farm today I try to give my best,
**R** esting at the end of the day on the hay.

**Dylan Vallance (7)**
Northlew And Ashbury Primary Parochial CE School, Okehampton

# Starry Space

**A** round the world countless times
**S** urrounded by darkness
**T** wisting and turning
**R** ockets flying by
**O** utside of my comfort zone
**N** othing to save me
**A** s I blast off for the last time
**U** nited with the stars
**T** ime stands still.

## Casper Page (10)
Northlew And Ashbury Primary Parochial CE School, Okehampton

# On The Farm

**T** ry to do my best at farming
**R** espect other people's machines
**A** pproaching a beautiful farm
**C** limbing up steps to a tractor cab
**T** ry to afford bigger machines
**O** n the farm today I try my best to help people
**R** esting at the end of the day.

**Zac Dryden (8)**
Northlew And Ashbury Primary Parochial CE School, Okehampton

# T-Rex's Size

**T** errifying creatures as big as buses.

**R** unning away like Usain Bolt.
**E** ven bigger than a massive boulder.
**X** -rays show just how big they are.

**Oliver Cork (9)**
Northlew And Ashbury Primary Parochial CE School, Okehampton

# In My Dreams

In my dreams,
I can't die.
In my dreams,
I can fly.
In my dreams,
I'm always fine.
In my dreams,
Life is divine.

**Laila Dryden-Chastey (9)**
Northlew And Ashbury Primary Parochial CE School, Okehampton

# Upside-Down Dreams

I went to bed as usual
I fell asleep as always
Soon, I began to dream that I was in a crowded shopping centre
All seemed normal until I looked up.

Above me, in place of the roof, was a zoo
Upside down
With upside-down animals
Walking around upside down
In their upside-down enclosures
I wondered whether they were real
Were they mirages? Tricks of the light?

Suddenly, the elongated neck of an inverted giraffe brushed past me
Definitely real
A tropical bird with radiant feathers fluttered above my head, the wrong way up
I could even feel a breeze as it whooshed past
This was not your standard zoo!

I tilted my head
Now it looked like the shopping centre was upside down
Maybe I was upside down
But I didn't feel like I was upside down.

The next thing I knew, I was falling
Upwards
Straight into the tortoise enclosure of the zoo
And then...
I was lying in bed.

It was a dream
The events of the past night had all taken place inside of my head
In my imagination.

But to this day, I have still not figured out which one was the right way up
Was it me, or the animals?

**Sophie B (11)**
South Moreton School, Didcot

# Nightmares

Rolling thunder, blue lightning, loneliness, plenty of loneliness
Ground shakes, trees shudder, the ground is a travesty
Blackness and I awoke.
Moving into another dream
Thunderstruck.

Running.
Running away from the past
Scared of the past, afraid of what had happened.
Endless running.
Moving into the abyss, perhaps I ought to stop
I know I must, but what will happen then?
Darkness.

My heart is grey; like a scrapyard, no emotions left.
Feelings destroyed, no desire, no nations, no creations, no populations.
All that but lonely, no stabs but stealthy, no rhymes at all
Heart is on fire, no mention of an extinguisher
Broken.

Black holes, sucking the world off like sweets
No way home now, in devastation.
All to see is the dark nothingness
Devastation.

Running away from the thunder that haunts the sky.
Broken, the damage the world has been through.
Devastation, the lightning that has destroyed trees and causes damage.
Dreams, curious dreams and this poem might just be one...
Awake.

**Alex Ackers (10)**
South Moreton School, Didcot

# In My Dream

It was a dark stormy night,
I woke up in my bed then I spotted a dark figure standing next to my door,
I was terrified,
But then I realised that I couldn't scream.
My thoughts were about how to wake up,
I spotted a light coming out from my door,
I stood up and pushed the dark figure next to the wall,
And went to the door.

After that, the world shifted,
Now I was in the long corridor with so many doors,
And one special door that said *Exit*.
I ran quickly to the door that said *Exit*, to check if it was locked or not.
"Oh no," it was locked, "I think there is a key somewhere in these doors."

When I opened the first door,
I saw... a void (nothing, just space but without stars).

When I opened the second door,
I saw... a lonely house in the middle of grass, sky and sun.

And in the third door, I found a chest,
When I opened it I saw... a *key*, finally.

I ran to the door that said *Exit*,
Put in the key and I entered.

I woke up.

**Sasha K (10)**
South Moreton School, Didcot

# The Cat Of Dreams

In the stillness of the night, a cat sits perched upon a cosy cloud in the cold twilight.
Its eyes glitter as it carefully watches a dream.
She watches, then secures her locket.

She pounces out of her soft skybox,
The night air whooshing throughout her black locks.
She wafts in the midnight breeze,
So quietly, you could even hear an ant sneeze.

The feline positions her silky paws and daintily descends to the stone rooftop, retracting her claws.
She elegantly saunters across the ridge,
As if she's walking on an unstable bridge.

She is graceful,
She is soft,
She is delicate.
She pounces into the boy's room and opens the locket, setting the dream free.
Into the mind it goes, locked and there is no key.

Her mission is done,
It's been and gone.
Her duty was served, yet not on a platter,
And all she hears is the rain's pitter-patter.
She's done her job, but there is no crowd,
But for now,
She'll admire her work, perched upon her cosy cloud.

**Cecily Hillegonds (11)**
South Moreton School, Didcot

# Bed

It was a dark night,
There was no light,
It became a test,
To get some rest,
Hitting the pillow,
I could feel my eyes getting low
I entered a deep, dark slumber,
It got darker and darker,
I was gone.

On a small, shadowy street,
A figure was pointing at me,
Unsure of what to do,
I started to run,
But whenever I looked, he was there,
The world shifted.

I entered a world of big doors,
All shapes and sizes,
Wondering what to do,
I tried, it wouldn't budge,
So I tried another door,
Nothing.
I started to panic,

I heard a groan and footsteps coming from a corridor,
Then I saw the beast,
It was giant, hairy and ugly,
Suddenly, the world shifted.

I found myself on a strange, blank island,
It was the abyss,
I woke up.

**James Aston (10)**
South Moreton School, Didcot

# Confusion In My Mind

I woke up in a dark gloomy room,
I could barely see any light.
The room appeared to be an office,
Its walls the colour of grey,
And a computer was there and it was square,
With eyes that stared into your soul.
And there was a dark, dusty door.
I couldn't want more to leave this dreaded place.
The door was surrounded by vines and I started to feel the signs.
The voice in my head said I needed to flee,
So I opened the door with no mis-er-e.

But to my surprise when I opened my eyes,
I hadn't moved a step.
I knew I had moved, I felt it in my feet,
But to my astonishment, the same place is what I meet.

I ran through that door again but I felt as if the world might end,
For I ended up in the same dark room.

**Enid Bonsu-Dartnall (11)**
South Moreton School, Didcot

# The Dream Of Me, Ramos

I had a dream that a football got stuck to my foot.
When I woke up from my dream, I was on a football pitch.
My bed was there too.
I saw a football so I kicked it as powerfully as possible.

The sticky football got stuck to my foot for five minutes.
I'd been trying to get it off.
A strange man appeared unexpectedly.
I was scared to death as he started to charge at me.
He looked like one of the most dangerous footballers of all time.
We called him Ramos.
When he edged by us, we numbered him four.

We called him Sergio Ramos.
When you'd see him your heart would turn to stone.
He was about three metres away from me.
He was going down to a slide tackle, studs up.
*Blackness!*

**Sonny Webster (11)**
South Moreton School, Didcot

# Another Dream...

After an uneventful day, my body craved rest
I felt my eyes slowly closing
As I gazed out wondering what was beyond the dark
Drifting into sleep, I felt myself falling
It was all a faint blur
Adjusting to the flashing lights in the distance
I realised where I was!

I was in a dream
As I whizzed through space, I came to a sudden stop
I could see a bizarre alien-looking creature peering strangely at me
I was frightened but seeing the kind smile he gave me, I decided to follow him.

We went on thrilling adventures through new universes
I knew that the fun would have to end somewhere
That's when I heard one of the snippy racer flies say,
"See you in your next dream!"

**Jessica C (10)**
South Moreton School, Didcot

# Dream Taker

The Dream Taker is a silent creeper
Who steals your souls like the Grim Reaper
You never see the thief that comes
Because he always eats up every crumb
Over time you feel empty and alone
It feels like your heart is turning to stone

Without a glance, he has a system
He stirs up fear and discontent
Slowly invades, his time well spent
The smell of death, his invention
The Dream Taker is a silent creeper
Who steals your souls like the Grim Reaper

Leaping from dream to dream
He always has a trick up his sleeve
Now he is starting to achieve
Now it's time for you to grieve
The Dream Taker is a silent creeper
Who steals your souls like the Grim Reaper.

**Cameron Rayner (10)**
South Moreton School, Didcot

# NJ Illusion

It was a dark and dusty night,
Exhausted, I urgently fell dead asleep.
Lifelessly, I saw figures.
Confused, scared.
Who? Where?

As I saw shadows of figures, they came closer and closer,
Blinking furiously.
Neymar Jr and Bellingham, right in front of my eyes.
Why were they here?

They slowed down.
Then they both started.
They were dancing to World Cup by Speed
A fire sparked everywhere!
Flames.

White, green, gold and blue flames flaming.
They started to burn my house down.
Smoke everywhere
It got hard to breathe and see.
Confused, scared.

Who? Where?
I thought we were at football.

I awoke, everything was a dream...

**Evie Bowler (10)**
South Moreton School, Didcot

# The Little Snowman

There was a little snowman, as white as can be
He had eyes made of rocks and arms from a tree
He liked cold winter days, but best of all
He loved to dream, he dreamed of everything
Even of summer, he thought dreaming was the most wonderful thing.

**Kaley Joseph (6)**
St John The Divine CE Primary School, Camberwell

# A Forest Mystery

**A** lways a wonder of what magical things might happen.
**D** aydreaming and *pow!* Magic has begun.
**V** enturing into the mysterious forest, blind to what might happen.
**E** ek! Brace yourselves, for the exit from the forest has closed! We have to escape!
**N** othing we can do but we have to move, for the Lunar Tiger is eyeing us up for a feast.
**T** ill morning comes, we have to hide in a deep, dark cave behind the vines.
**U** naware of what we might see, we have to go and flee.
**R** un! Run! The exit has opened. Who knows, we might have won the lucky token.
**E** ntering back into the land of the living, realising it was just a magical dream.

**Milena Katherine Lawrence (11)**
St Joseph's Primary School, Gabalfa

# Dreaming Of Walt Disney World

**W** alt Disney World, where dreams come true.
**A** s magical as can be.
**L** iving with the princesses.
**T** ag along and you will see.

**D** umbo, Donald, Dopey and Daisy.
**I** nvite you to ride along with them.
**S** plash, space and thunder mountain.
**N** ew adventures every day.
**E** nchanting parades and firework displays.
**Y** ou will never feel bored.

**W** ill anyone be able to pull King Arthur's sword?
**O** ne-of-a-kind characters like Mickey Mouse.
**R** iding roller coasters and the haunted house.
**L** osing track as time gets swirled.
**D** reaming of Walt Disney World.

## Millie O'Brien (10)
St Joseph's Primary School, Gabalfa

# A Nightmare...

**A** s I walk along the dread grass,

**N** othing to see except some rats.
**I** wonder why I'm in this strange place,
**G** lancing around thinking there's going to be a chase.
**H** igh and low I look around, and then I see a scary clown!
**T** hinking this is a mean joke, I run like Usain Bolt.
**M** oving non-stop, I feel like I'm going to drop!
**A** manic smile spreads across his terrible face.
**R** andom spiders also join the chase!
**E** ven though it's just a dream, it always makes me want to scream.

**Joanne Ifada (10)**
St Joseph's Primary School, Gabalfa

# One Dark Room

Scary and dark all around,
Not even in a corner is there sound,
I take a step forward,
From me, there is no word,
I look to my right, darkness covers,
I look to my left, only darkness' powers,
I want to cry in this eerie place,
Suddenly I feel the urge to escape,
I push myself forward and start to run,
Then I find myself suddenly stunned,
I slowly lose the ability to speak,
No part of me I can tweak,
I try to hold back the tears,
Soon I woke up to find it was all a nightmare,
Where I faced one of my fears.

**Drishya Babu (10)**
St Joseph's Primary School, Gabalfa

# My Magical Dream

Once upon a dream...
The ocean was a magical potion,
That used motion to create its waves.
I lay on the beach reaching,
For a peach, to give one to my parents each.
I saw a snail riding a whale,
With a magnificent tail.
I played with shells,
Which sounded like bells,
And had some funny smells.
The warm sand was the strand
Of land in my hand.
When I cruised in my boat,
I cooked some Scottish oats,
And wore a rainbow coat,
Once upon a dream.

**Maurycy Hebel (10)**
St Joseph's Primary School, Gabalfa

# Dreams

**D** reaming is something wonderful - it is your own world.
**R** unning like Usain Bolt, flying like a falcon - anything is possible in this weird and wonderful world.
**E** normous insects, tiny animals - you can imagine anything in this world of yours.
**A** lmost to the exciting bit, then your world fades away.
**M** ost dreams are brilliant but nightmares are your darkest worlds.
**S** weet dreams!

**Pranav Shake (10)**
St Joseph's Primary School, Gabalfa

# The Dead Field

The roses were beautiful, the sunset looked good too!
But that all changed. Nothing had prepared me for this dream
I saw a three-headed clown running at me, it was all I could see...
The beautiful sunset turned into a rainy storm
The fresh roses turned into dead flowers
The clown almost got me...
But then I woke up
To find myself safe inside my bed!

**Ruby-Rose Stacey (10)**
St Joseph's Primary School, Gabalfa

# Dreamland

I closed my eyes and swept into wonder,
Skies in a dreamland all of wonder and surprise.
In this place, I loved to be,
Dreamland, full of friends and fantasy.
I can fly in the sky way, way up high,
Give me a wave as I go by.
In my dream, I can be anything I want to be,
This is what makes Dreamland my favourite place to be!

**Alysia Jones Pleace (10)**
St Joseph's Primary School, Gabalfa

# Leap

Last night, I fell asleep
I saw a unicorn doing a leap
Starlight tails and moonlight beams
One by one, they passed me
Glancing left and right
All I saw was starlight
Now I woke up in my bed
Maybe I will see them next year.

**Gracie Toppar (11)**
St Joseph's Primary School, Gabalfa

# The Silver Lynx

Most nights, in my bizarre and broken dreams,
I am presented as a silver lynx, watching over icy streams,
I would meander through beautiful forests of snow,
Climbing over mountains which would gleam and glow.

The sparkling sun would shine over my silky fur,
And I would lie down, just to sit and purr,
I'd jump around and wander through waterfalls,
Tossing through rivers like an ashen doll.

I know I don't have paws, I have hands and feet,
But these dreams make me free, I'd become them in a heartbeat!
I can still crawl around, on all fours,
But anyway these lucid dreams, they give me paws!

When the night arrives, my animal comes awake,
And the rules of reality are ones I can break!
Although it stays chained up in day,
The moon's arrival stops its lonely dismay.

It usually ends in a shower of snowflakes,
And yet, they would know, and their heart would ache.
I look forward to every night - the freedom, the immunity,
And I know deep inside, my silver lynx and I are in unity.

**Olivia Timms (11)**
St Mary's Catholic Primary School, Newcastle-Under-Lyme

# Trophy Of Life

**T** hrough highs and lows, I'll keep going,
**R** ich with encouragement, I'll keep exploring.
**O** pportunity is everywhere, I'll keep chasing,
**P** ride in achievements, I'll keep winning.
**H** onour for family, I'll keep building,
**Y** oung me will keep inspiring.

**O** ffering my success to God and parents will be my victory,
**F** or in their love, my success finds the key.

**L** ife is like a journey, I'll never get tired,
**I** n the dream where my future is my trophy, with pride.
**F** ulfilling my dream is what I want to earn,
**E** very day is an opportunity to learn.

**Pita Joseph Rhys Ezekiel Daniel Smith-Tavakece (10)**
St Mary's Catholic Primary School, Newcastle-Under-Lyme

# The Park

When I was at the park,
I saw trees made out of bark,
I went on the slide, swings and monkey bars,
I also met with my friend, whose name is Cart.

**Connor Jordan (10)**
St Mary's Catholic Primary School, Newcastle-Under-Lyme

# Mysterious Land

**M** y mind goes heavy as I drift off to sleep,
**Y** earning for a sleep that's deep.
**S** cared, I find myself sleeping. I look around and
**T** hink, *this is not my house?! What have I found?*
**E** ventually, I think this is the dream I had, "I'm in my dream!"
**R** ealising everything, I shout in excitement, but wait, there's something strange.
**I** walk and walk until I hear a voice, but a sweet voice.
**O** n a blue ledge, there was a box which had my name.
**U** nder the box was something strange.
**S** omething unusual, like a little fairy.

**L** aying down but not just any fairy; a lava fairy.
**A** nd a water woman, lying next to her and more people.
**N** oticing that they were trapped, I knew I had to save them but
**D** anger lurks around everywhere I go...

**Vygha Jismon (10)**
St Mungo's RC Primary School, Alloa

# Galaxy Runway

Tonight me and my friends are going to Dubai,
Honestly, I might cry.
We got on a plane and we were off!
Then I had a cough.
We were starting to head up and I had the window seat,
Once we were there, I wondered who we'd meet.

We buckled our seat and off we went.
But from the cabin, I heard the snore
Of a dinosaur that needed to *roar!*
I closed my window and had a sleep,
And I woke up to a *beep!*

Everyone was screaming! What had happened?
I looked out of the window...
Galaxies and dragons, planets and stars, cows and chickens!
We were leaving the Milky Way
And I saw a planet shaped like Santa's sleigh.

We had to pray to be okay.
"Hey, hey! Wake up! Time for school!"
Time to wake up,
It is a rule!

**Connor Clark (10)**
St Mungo's RC Primary School, Alloa

# SpongeBob Dream

**S** o dreams can be scary
**P** eople can have dreams relating to them
**O** n the other hand, I dream about SpongeBob
**N** ow, before you say SpongeBob is just a sponge with a job, he is
**G** reat
**E** very night I dream about SpongeBob
**B** ut one dream was different so let me tell you about it
**O** n this occasion, SpongeBob came to visit me
**B** ut why?

"**D** anger, danger," he said
"**R** escue Patrick, quick!"
**E** ven though I was
**A** fraid, I did
**M** orning! I'll probably never have a dream like that ever again.

### Stephen Moore (10)
St Mungo's RC Primary School, Alloa

# The Dad Monster

**M** e, myself, in my bed.
**O** h, there's something at my door...
**N** o, it's not something, it's someone!
**S** taring at me from the corner of his eye!
**T** errified, I tiptoed out of bed, trying to get past him.
**E** agerly, I gave him a little poke; I don't think he liked that!
**R** udely, I gave a giant, blood-curdling scream! He then turned the light on.

"**D** ad! Dad!" I screamed, giving him a big hug!
**A** nd then he rudely gave me a poke. "Hey!" I said.
**D** ad said, "Payback!" Then I woke up in bed. What a dream!

**Khloe Holdsworth (10)**
St Mungo's RC Primary School, Alloa

# Beautiful Dogs

**B** eautiful dogs. I love Weimaraners. They are cute.
**E** veryone is nice to my dog. She is very cute.
**A** nywhere I go with my dog she always jumps on people. It's funny!
**U** sually she bites playfully and acts like a dinosaur...
**T** hey are very big dogs which I like because they can keep the house safe.
**I** n my house she always eats anything, even me!
**F** orgiving my dog every time because when she looks at you, you can't resist giving her a pat on the head.
**U** sually she sleeps after long walks
**L** ove my dog but the long walks are tiring!

**Gabriella Annabell Czarnik (10)**
St Mungo's RC Primary School, Alloa

# The Galaxy Plane

Tonight was my big long flight.
I went on the plane and put my seatbelt on tight.
The lady came over and she was really polite.
I knew we were going to Spain, but we weren't!
In reality, we were going to the galaxy.
The lady said, "Can you move over?"
So I said, "Alright."
We were about to reach the galaxy.
One hour later we did, it was really dark.
I saw I had a mark on my arm.
I saw cars were parked.
The cars were floating in the air.
I said, "I made it, just can't hate it."

**Aron Beely (10)**
St Mungo's RC Primary School, Alloa

# Nightmare

Lurking in the dark a fearful sight
Only comes on the darkest night
With amber eyes glowing bright
You're unlucky if you catch sight
With sharp pointy teeth
He lives beneath
All the heaps of clothes
I always wonder when he goes
With his ragged robe and crooked nose
As he contemplates his next move as the brisk wind blows
As he moves through the house
As quiet as a mouse
As night grows into dawn
He runs away like a fawn
As I rise from my bed
And he has already fled.

**Grace Gallagher (10)**
St Mungo's RC Primary School, Alloa

# The Magical Writer!

I'm here in my room as I read and write.
My mind bursts with ideas, late into the night.
When all goes silent, I write at my best.
My pencil doesn't stop, it never takes a rest.

I sit and dream of being a writer one day.
Signing my own books, what can I say?
Someday this poem may be published and will sell.
No one really knows, only time will tell.

In the meantime, I'll dream and be excited.
And one day, I'll be known as a writer who was knighted!

**Olivia Hall (9)**
St Mungo's RC Primary School, Alloa

# Bigfoot Chase

**N** ever had I thought I'd be here now.
**I** kind of wonder how.
**G** et me home and make it fast
**H** opefully, I can last.
**T** *hump! Thump! Thump!* It's Bigfoot in the middle of the dump.
**M** um, where are you? I screamed
**A** s Bigfoot opened his mouth and his ears steamed
**R** unning fast, then I gasp, on an
**E** mpty stomach. Bigfoot picked me up.
**S** uddenly, I woke up with a headache.

**Jacob Lovell (10)**
St Mungo's RC Primary School, Alloa

# Magical Dancers

Magical dancers' glowing eyes.
In my room tonight.
Beautiful wings and flexible legs.
Twirling and lifting their sequin skirts.
One by one they make a circle.
Prancing along, little legs.
I hear the music, I now wake up.
I open my eyes, I feel confused.
They stop and freeze, they disappear.
I collect the dust and close my eyes.
I drift asleep. Come back next year, magical dancers.

**Emmie Douglas (9)**
St Mungo's RC Primary School, Alloa

# Scary Dreams

**N** ight-time is a scary time.
**I** had a dream I was with my bro in the snow.
**G** iant clowns were chasing me!
**H** ad me in his arms. *Argh!*
**T** oo late to escape...
**M** aybe I can beat him up?
**A** nd report him to the police.
**R** eally want this dream to end!
**E** ventually, I woke up and it was morning. *Phew!*

**Jensen McAdam (10)**
St Mungo's RC Primary School, Alloa

# In The Bernabéu

**A** lmost fainting with the people I see,
**C** ristiano Ronaldo, Marcelo and me,
**R** unning on their pitch is a dream I've had,
**O** n the pitch with Ramos, he's such a lad.
**S** printing on the pitch, I scream
**"T** o your right!" I hope they hear me,
**I** n the box, I run in,
**C** ristiano crosses, I hit the top bins.

**Harry Douglas (10)**
St Mungo's RC Primary School, Alloa

# Sprinkle Land

**D** ancing ducks with flying dogs and my cat flying.
**R** ainbow cats in frosty frosting caves, cuddly and cute!
**E** xcited I am, I tasted the ground; it tasted good!
**A** golden retriever playing like a beaver.
**M** oonlight with meteorites, people piped in the night.
**S** prinkle Land will expand; well you may be tanned.

**Nadia Ludwiczak (10)**
St Mungo's RC Primary School, Alloa

# The Journey

I close my eyes and begin to dream...
I see myself in a football team.
Playing in green against the Hearts,
About to break all the fans' hearts.
Getting scouted by Barcelona.
Playing like present Al Nassr,
Signing a five-year contract years ago,
It was a dream, not fact.
Astonished I made it! Just can't hate it.

**Max Cassidy (10)**
St Mungo's RC Primary School, Alloa

# Untitled

**S** nowmen dancing with the reindeer,
**N** o one was awake. Very late
**O** n a snowy mountain I see the
**W** riters packing away all their gear
**M** ittens hang outside to play in the snow
**A** ngels flying along beautifully
**N** aughty kids crying because they're getting cold.

**Alix Lawrie (10)**
St Mungo's RC Primary School, Alloa

# Gymnastics

**G** roups of teams
**Y** es I am ready
**M** aybe you can like it too
**N** eed to practise more
**A** nd we help each other
**S** o one, two. One, two, three let's go!
**T** o have fun!
**I** love gymnastics
**C** ome along and have fun
**S** o yes, bye!

**Lilly Kane (10)**
St Mungo's RC Primary School, Alloa

# A Nightmare

**N** ever-ending room
**I** n my head
**G** iglesaurus comes to life
**H** e's chasing me
**T** he room never ends
**M** y head wants it to end
**A** door up ahead
**R** oar! I hear
**"E** veryone help me!" I scream.

**Perri Starkey (10)**
St Mungo's RC Primary School, Alloa

# Magical Fairies

**F** airies fly in the morning sky,
**A** way so far up high.
**I** see them using their magical powers,
**R** eally, it's true!
**I** 'm always excited!
**E** very one is a different shape and size.
**S** anguinely, they come again.

**Alba Williamson (10)**
St Mungo's RC Primary School, Alloa

# Clones From Star Wars

**C** lones from Star Wars battle the battle droids on Naboo (a Star Wars planet)
**L** aughs come from the clones on the ship
**O** h no! Lord Tom comes to the ship door
**N** ow Lord Tom opens the door
**E** veryone prepares for battle.

**Logan Cameron (9)**
St Mungo's RC Primary School, Alloa

# Bikini Bottom

Me and my friend sit on a ship.
The ship starts to tip.
We are heading to Dubai,
And I think I'm going to die!
I take a big sigh.
I then say goodbye.
Now I'm in the ocean.
It's Bikini Bottom!

**Kai McMorrow (10)**
St Mungo's RC Primary School, Alloa

# Abandoned Village

An abandoned village, extremely old.
No people live in a place so cold.
All the trees are beginning to die.
The breezy, cold wind makes an extremely loud sigh.
All the roofs are covered in moss like a glazed doughnut.
Since all the trees are dead, there is not one growing coconut.

Dusty cobwebs in every corner.
So cold that it's frozen over.
The opposite of a hot steam sauna.

A scary bug in every nook and cranny.
Such an old creaky plank, it's older than my great-granny!
Such a huge shadow, I lost my sanity.
This one tiny house was absolutely petrifying me!
I felt so sick, I thought I was stranded at sea.
I felt spiders on my arms and they were wet and soggy.
Then, I woke up!
And it turned out the soggy spiders were my dog, Foggy.

**Viraaj Singh Kalsi (8)**
Sundon Lower School, Upper Sundon

# Once Upon A Dream

Once in my dream,
I saw fruits and vegetables.
The sweet raspberries were beautiful flowers,
The squeezy oranges were rolling balls,
And we could juggle with them too.
The white cauliflowers were puffy clouds,
The sour lemon was a bright sun.
The funny bananas were telephones to call our best friends,
The crunchy carrots were shooting
Like flying rockets.
The pineapple was a big hut
For the blueberry bees.
Finally, the delicious fruits and vegetables were turning into a nice, healthy house.
I had so much fun and yum in my dream.

**Davina Dencil (7)**
Sundon Lower School, Upper Sundon

# My Football Space Dream Adventure

Mum, I dreamt I was in space last night,
The stars were shining ever so bright.
In the distance, Earth was there,
Squinting at the sun's powerful glare.

I was floating on Planet Jupiter.
I met a green alien called Zoolafer,
We played the best football together,
With rock as light as a feather.
Lots of flicks and tricks in the air,
Keepy-uppies on Earth could never compare.

Stripy, swirly, whirly Jupiter,
Large, cold, bold, peculiar.
Suddenly, back with a *boom*,
Wide awake in my room!

**Jeevan Bhaker (8)**
Sundon Lower School, Upper Sundon

# Superpowers

Like a snowglobe, quietly floating free,
I see scared little children just like me.
Falling from the cold, misty sky,
The frightened children begin to cry.

There is disastrous evil gliding above,
An out-of-space galaxy in need of love.
As fast as a jet, lightning strikes by,
Powerful superheroes begin to fly.

Flashes of light beam from their eyes,
The dangerous villains are in for a surprise!
Slowly as a feather, the children hit the ground,
We are all safe, celebrations all around.

**Nico Charles (9)**
Sundon Lower School, Upper Sundon

# Cup Final

Floodlights illuminate the lush, green pitch
The town crowd roar my name
Bossing midfield and scoring great goals is the way
I play my game.
Trickery, flickery, flip flaps
And a nutmeg to spice up the cup final match
Running rings around the opposition team
Beating each man.
A shot from forty yards
The best goal Wembley has ever seen.
Giving my all until
The whistle blows and the ref signals full-time.
Climbing the steps to lift the cup
A winner's medal will be mine.

**Jason Roe (8)**
Sundon Lower School, Upper Sundon

# The Old Mansion

An enchanted mansion
With a golden bedroom
The ceiling curved with patterns.
Gold, blue and silver shone
In the daylight.

Two lions on the doorstep
Waiting for their prey
Hundreds of birds sitting upon them.

Thousands of green lights
In the corridors
One light followed by happiness.

Music on a harp
The mansion turned into a cottage
With a mossy roof, there were happy people.

**Roxanne Janas (7)**
Sundon Lower School, Upper Sundon

# Imagination

**I** will always be me
**M** e, entering a competition
**A** gain, I'm floating in the air
**G** oing on a colourful rainbow
**I** n giant marshmallows with Nutella in them
**N** avigating to end up in Candy Cane Lane
**A** bove the highest clouds jumping
**T** apping and everyone dancing
**I** end up magically dancing
**O** n top of the Eiffel Tower!
**N** ow, I'm tap dancing!

**Saffiya Charles (9)**
Sundon Lower School, Upper Sundon

# Sweet Treats

Once upon a dream
In a land beyond the trains' steam
I'd dream of sweet treats
Jelly beans, sour pops and lollipops I wish to eat
Bursting flavours tickled my tongue
Making me feel so young
Long red laces fluttered into my mouth like shooting stars
Picking cola cubes, toffees and lemon sherbets out of a jar
Take me high into the cotton candy clouds
Where a whole enchanted world is calling out aloud.

**Haajer Sadiq (8)**
Sundon Lower School, Upper Sundon

# Monsters

**M** unching and crunching their way through the fairground.
**O** range, angry eyes all around.
**N** obody is with me and I'm very scared.
**S** harp teeth and claws and all colourful hair.
**T** he size of an eagle, they fly looking for prey.
**E** veryone is running away!
**R** apidly the rain begins to fall.
**S** hrinking the monsters to the size of a ping pong ball!

**Stefan Gagic (8)**
Sundon Lower School, Upper Sundon

# There Was A Day In Storyland

There was a day in Storyland,
Where the people were happy and sad.
There was a day in Storyland,
Where Peter Pan was sick.
There was a day in Storyland,
When the Gingerbread Man ran away.
The problem was... it was the same day!
So the fox ate the Gingerbread Man,
Captain Hook gave Peter Pan some special soup
And the Three Little Pigs cheered the people up.

**Felix Orme (8)**
Sundon Lower School, Upper Sundon

# Sweet World

Here in my sweet world,
I eat a candy cane until I feel a tummy ache,
I stuff my mouth with sweets.
As I watch the candy clouds fly from the south,
As I eat gummy bears and sour straws,
I realise I'm in a candy wonderland without flaws.
As I go to shore, I see a chocolate raft,
As I take a bite, I sink into this very sweet dream.

**Riya Sharma (8)**
Sundon Lower School, Upper Sundon

# My First Day

Will they like me?
Will I make friends?
Will they let me play?
Will I get lost and not find my way?
What will my teachers be like?
Will the work be hard?
Will the food be nice?
I hope we play games in the yard.

Well I had a good day
I made loads of mates
Then school was finished
I met my mum at the gates.

**Mia-Rose Garland (7)**
Sundon Lower School, Upper Sundon

# Football

**F** rom when I close my eyes
**O** pen fields is what I see
**O** range T-shirts fill the pitch
**T** en children feeling happy
**B** alls flying in the air
**A** dults watching in a line
**L** ights from the sun are coming through
**L** ittle children running on the pitch.

**Harrison Martin (9)**
Sundon Lower School, Upper Sundon

# Sweet Dreams

Candyfloss fills the sky,
Milkshake river flows on by.
Ice cream covering the mountain tops,
The heavens open with mint choc raindrops.
Doughnut boulders rolling down the hills,
Jelly beans fly for they love to chill.
Flying saucers come and go,
Where does it all stop?
No one knows.

**James Price (7)**
Sundon Lower School, Upper Sundon

# Candy Lane

My Candy Cane Lane dream is stripy red and white
Tasty, full of delight.
My house is made of candy, fluffy, bright and full of fun,
Tasting of peppermint, bubblegum and all things yum.
Next time I hope I dream of rainbows and pots of gold.

**Ah'Shay Duncan (8)**
Sundon Lower School, Upper Sundon

# YOUNG WRITERS INFORMATION

We hope you have enjoyed reading this book – and that you will continue to in the coming years.

If you're a young writer who enjoys reading and creative writing, or the parent of an enthusiastic poet or story writer, do visit our website **www.youngwriters.co.uk**. Here you will find free competitions, workshops and games, as well as recommended reads, a poetry glossary and our blog.

If you would like to order further copies of this book, or any of our other titles, then please give us a call or visit **www.youngwriters.co.uk**.

Young Writers
Remus House
Coltsfoot Drive
Peterborough
PE2 9BF
(01733) 890066
info@youngwriters.co.uk

**YoungWritersUK**   **YoungWritersCW**
**youngwriterscw**   **youngwriterscw**